HIJITO

———

Broken River Prize winner, 2018
selected by Eduardo C. Corral

Grace & Gabriel—this book,
and everything, is for you.

Introduction

At a time of crisis and fragmentation in this country, we need poets who will see our common humanity and speak to that humanity without resorting to the dead language of cliché. At a time when violence in this society is not only epidemic but enormously profitable, we need poets who will speak out against violence in all its manifestations, from the internalized lessons of youth to the brute force of the state. At a time when racial stereotypes—slandering those of Latin American origin or descent—influence social policy and public opinion in the U.S., we need poets whose very existence erases such stereotypes. In short, we need poets like Carlos Andrés Gómez.

The reader or listener encountering the poems in *Hijito* might expect this poet to recall his own experiences with street violence in general and gun violence in particular. Indeed, by fifteen he had seen too much, and would go on to witness a dear friend broken in a flash of rage; by twenty-three, as a social worker in Harlem, he would save a pimp from being shot by an irate john, coming perilously close to taking the bullet himself in the bargain. These poems are visceral, the stinging slap of memory jolting us awake.

However, what the reader or listener would never anticipate is the leap from such quotidian violence in this country—birthed in the blood of conquest—to the horrors of the genocide in Rwanda, as the poet does in two indelible poems contained herein. This is the kind of leap that requires vision, and, indeed, this poet is a visionary humanist, seeing bridges where others see only the deepest of waters, a spectrum of violence met with resistance to violence, a commitment to peace through poetry that goes beyond the rhetoric of peace practiced by those in power.

Through it all, Carlos Andrés Gómez navigates the meanings of Latino maleness in an age when President Trump whips his minions into a fury over the "bad hombres" menacing the fragile borders of the United States. Whether he writes of his father or himself as a father, in poem after poem, this poet asks the tough question: *what is a man?* The answer, invariably, springs from a commitment to changing the world.

That he meets these challenges with strong images and lyrical grace is extraordinary. As he says in his poem, "Morning, Riker's Island," about the adolescents incarcerated there: "here's the miracle: / the sun frees everyone / to sing." The words of this poet free everyone to sing. As Brecht put it: "In the dark times / Will there also be singing? / Yes, there will also be singing / About the dark times." All we have to do now is listen.

Martín Espada
June, 2019

hijito

[ee-*hee*-toe]

Spanish, diminutive and/or endearment form of *son* or *child*.

Hijito

for Michael Brown

I am enthralled by the image
in front of me: my face overlaid
with his—a boy, almost a man, inside
the glass of a grocery store
reaching for a branch
of seedless grapes.

This sly mirror. This taut mirage.
A coiling limb slithers in my gut, its roots
(invisible)—like I am on this asphalt
to any soul that is inside, right now,
like he is. Today, she is
nine weeks along, he is almost eighteen,
and I am grasping for any thought
that is not my son calling out breathless
from the hollow lungs of night, abandoned
seven feet from the hood of a patrol car
where a hubcap swallows secrets
beside a pavement-choked throat
heaving for breath (his jawline borrowed
from my face). Above it, a still-shaking
hand crowned by smoke uniformed
in my skin.

I

Poem about Death
Ending with Reincarnation

after Matthew Olzmann & Tarfia Faizullah

Blood has its own democracy.
My father & I puncture steaks
& watch them ooze—deep maple
walls eavesdrop as steel teeth

scrape & claw the porcelain
we use to distract our manically
clenching jaws. I'm well-practiced
in this ritual: empty & fill, empty

& fill, until there's nothing.
Our filets gone, we sit & stare
at the eggshell table spread,
abdomens swelling like silence—

They found a mass.
She's having surgery next week.
I had always planned for him
to be first. Now the woman

fifteen years his junior, mother
to my twin baby siblings, is dying
or might be. I've been rehearsing
years for this talk, except it isn't—

my father, held only by the dim
lighting that shrouds his silhouette,
reduced to heaving. I envision
the stepmom it took me eleven years

to embrace being lowered carefully
into the damp earth, an old man,
flanked by two teenagers, watching,
& I will be there too: an overcast

Tuesday that no one passing by
will remember, & as usual, I won't
be able to get the dimple right
in my tie. For a second, although

we are nowhere near the mountains,
I will smell the crisp air she so
loved & remember the first time
we walked without the heaviness

of that first encounter both of us
carried for far too long. But on that
unremarkable day for most, a light
rain will interrupt the hike I am on

in my mind, a man will read overly-
rehearsed words from a book she
did not believe in, & we will stand
like guards, numb. We will watch over

the sacred earth she spent an entire
lifetime trying to protect, now her
home, flanked by roots cross-stitching
the rich soil, what becomes the promise

kept to those endless rows of buds
ready to push through & that twisted
symmetry just above, a dangled blade
from a mouth chewing in first light.

Kigali Memorial

Superman sheets hang in the genocide memorial
identical to the ones I had in middle school—hid
from my first girlfriend as we trafficked kisses,
afraid she might discover I was still a boy.

My thirteen-year-old self confronts this hero,
his rippled body rising, always rising towards
something I could never see, arms outstretched
in endless flight, or was it a kind of surrender?

Eye-level with the youth I outgrew,
fingertips pressed against glass, warm
as a father's yawning throat, its unconscious grace.
As the air in my chest thins, I imagine someone

taking my covers and smuggling them to this hill
in East Africa, my adolescence abruptly erased.
What was I so busied with that incessant April?
How many souls perished each time I blinked?

I sift murmurs for the voice of the boy
trapped inside the monument now ensnaring me.
I picture someone inside my ribcage, knitting a scroll
of names. I am fifty-three feet from the Exit,

a small doorway with a low arch that opens
into a lush pasture where 258,000 people
and me, a seventh grader, stretch endlessly
into dust. The sunrays that spill through

the fissure in this room bear light that darkens
the shadows already being cast. The contrast
so stark that parts of the room suddenly disappear
and, for a moment, everything—my childhood

sheets, the strangers' huddled weeping,
photographs of families stacked floor to ceiling,
my restless hands, babies' shoes, an identity
card smeared with blood—is gone.

Pronounced

You excavate anything that has tried to lodge itself
in your body without permission. You bury the toothbrush
between your back molars and scrape whatever

you find. One loss makes you feel all other losses.
Eleven years later, when you no longer eat pizza
or speak Spanish, when your father's profile invades

your clenched jawline, you borrow his brisk gait,
his snort, his face. People say you look white.
Your father never does. The restaurant won't seat

you, the hostess says neither of you meet the dress
code (your father's wearing a double-breasted suit).
You are a man trying to roll your *rs* again. Where did

the words go? You are still trying to retrieve the sounds
you once dreamt in. You hardly remember your mother
tongue. You are trying to pull something useable from

the wreckage. Yet it all feels familiar. Your best friend
compliments your clean pronunciation, the way you have
learned to let go of everything you once called home.

The Afternoon You Moved Out

In our lopsided driveway
that would lure my basketball towards
the busy street, I was shooting
hoops on a seven-foot rim.
You pulled my limp arms
around your waist and told me
the one thing that would make me
stop crying: *I won't make us move
again*. And then gone. I don't

remember the bag you must have
dragged half-open across the lawn
I had forgotten to cut the afternoon
before, or the way my sister must have
sat, turned her radio up as loud as
possible and then watched from
the second-floor window. None of
those memories stick. They are empty

boxes like the cardboard we would
assemble every year or two and use
to hoard more and more bad drawings
and the clothes our cousins had passed
down. I wonder if my daughter will
remember I read to her every single
day I ever spent with her. Or if she
will only remember the times I was

not there: the field hockey game
I might miss in sixth grade, when
prom coincides with a conference
I have no choice but to attend, or
that moment she calls from college
and needs me. I remember the rare
days better than all the others,
cannot recall what you said

before the car door closed, only
the house still haunted
by the endless rolls of half-used
packing tape, the same tape I used
to take lint off the dress shirt Mommy
had picked for class pictures.

Black Hair

I made a vow
        to join clustered
strands with these
        fingers, careful
as they are clumsy,
        submerged in this
delicate calculus.
        I learn about
love doing this,
        preparing for some-
one who might
        help me understand
all of this better.
        I keep starting
over, as though
        concentration
is where I took
        my misstep, as though
I am not three decades
        behind in my practice.
As though it is just
        a pattern I'm trying
to find (too late).
        I'm too late, I think,
or maybe it's something else: Papi's hands
        never knew how to fix
my sister's hair. I tend to
        each thick, onyx strand

like I'm mending
        her favorite cardigan,
as though my calloused
        hands might coax and
shape anything into an
        ordered grace. I layer
another braid across
        my love's scalp.
I can feel, with each
        pull and twist, the newly
assembled crib watching.

Edge of the Dance Floor

after Terrance Hayes

What? Are you
a faggot? she asked. My palm
    offered like a fist

    of tulips—*a man takes*
what he wants—as the bassline
    flooded our bodies

    into a starved harmony
of salt. I clawed her waist, the nearest
    corner swallowing

    us whole as her head
tumbled towards a cemetery of three-
    day-old beer. In the epileptic

    surge of strobe, she looked
woman, as all the boys smiled,
    fanged in stage smoke.

    We were told nothing
was off-limits. A shy kid
    in oversized jeans un-

    snapped the bra of the fresh-
man just within reach. None of us survived
    that night. We stand forever

on a precipice
we did not choose, glance back
at the mirages

we became. My eyes
were better closed, fear in the hull
of my gut—all I see now:

a sprawl of men carrying
the ache we recognize better
than the men whose names

we borrow, the grief
umbilical. The night my child was
born, the cord refused

our baby that first heavy gulp
of breath, heartbeat dissipating into
a tapestry of mechanical sounds.

I thought life was the only
question—heavy as an ancient anchor on
my lungs—until my body sighed

as though the gun jammed
next to my temple when I found out
my child was not a boy.

What Happened

We all know what happened. But
let's say we left the bar four minutes
earlier, by the time it would have
happened we were already in the car.

Let's say we skipped the pair
of birthday shots from the mouthy
bartender. We'd have made
it home, right? Or, let's say I was

seventeen feet closer when
it happened. Say the car
keys somehow found their
way into my hands, I blink,

we're home. Or we
don't make it, I blink again,

we're singed metal across
the median, couldn't make the hard
pull off the Franklin exit. I live. He

doesn't. Or worse: he does. Whatever
is left of him.

We remember the story
we commit to. Then, we tell
ourselves it happened.

Whatever happened: we were celebrating.
All good and well. But let's say, I'd just
broken up with my girlfriend or didn't have
a reason to live.

Let's say I was three inches shorter, or spent
more time measuring the symmetry of
my face, waded through long evenings
with a bottle of Jack Daniels against
my chin pretending it was a pistol.

Later that night, say I'd told the police officer
in the basement of Vanderbilt Medical Center I had
a description. Given a vague account of the guy
and it led to seven random Black men
in East Nashville—on the way to the pharmacy

for cigarettes or diapers or Skittles or
chemotherapy medication—getting locked up.

One gets seven years. A kid loses her father.

Let's say I was standing by Brent's side
when it happened and not across
the street, buzzed and fuming with
my back turned, while he dragged ass
and drunk-called the first pretty
face in his phone.

Say he didn't have eyelashes no one
can look away from, didn't respond
to the guy's girlfriend as she called
out. Say the fist didn't arrive more quickly
than the moment.

Let's say it wasn't his birthday. We played
another game of one-on-one that afternoon,
one of us sprained our ankle (probably him).
Or I got food poisoning: the lunch buffet
had a bad piece of butter chicken.

I'm not saying I believe in fate or religion.
Or anything. But let's say only one of us
survives.

The guy took another swing, then
another, then used his boot like an axe on the concrete curb.
Or what if a knife came out or a twenty-two.

                He looked like the cartoon of a guy
                trying too hard. A guy no one takes
                seriously, then shows up to work
                in body armor with an AR-15.

                I know what happened, endlessly:

    We leave   start to walk up   street and towards

next to the   hotel or maybe it was a building that looked like   and
    I'm
in front of him, or maybe, at first, we were side-by-side up the

hill. It was early   , and   was out that night.
                It was a few minutes after   o'clock in the
morning, or just before. Definitely close to the hour. I'm sure of that.

        called out first to   .   and they're chest-to-chest

someone   it sounded   like the crack of a wooden   against

concrete   and he just   like a redwood felled

suv blocked   EMT smelled like cigarettes   I think maybe
he was smoking?   and he keeps asking the same question

MRI   the same question   fifty-seven staples down his skull

        same question   I drive home   seven hours later, hands still
shaking   dried blood
        changed the color of my button down   off-white to dark

        burgundy.

        the same question   the   walks   same   in

    the doorway   question

flight   phone call

                                his parents   same

          question   the curtains   stayed drawn   months.

II

Mein Kampf has better reviews
than *One Hundred Years of Solitude*

on Amazon—I found out today,
at the exact moment a sound
like drowning (or heaving) took me
and my ears hostage, as a kerfuffle
of futile scrapping tried desperately
to keep a bird atop a ledge, so as not
to tumble from my fifth-floor air conditioner.

I could tell you: *Nature is breathtaking*
or carefully describe how the scent
of my daughter's sweat-dampened
scalp, just after she's woken and taken
that long drawl of a yawn, is still cradled
by the pillow on my lap where her nape
was resting just sixteen minutes ago, but
what would that prove?

Once, I watched a slight, nervous man
in a starched, pressed uniform empty
a flurry of baton hits on the limp skull
of a homeless man for snatching
a rich woman's purse. Watching, I felt freed
of my innocence, all seven and a half
years of my life seemed to evaporate
into the thick summer air of Central Park.
It was 1989 and I knew, definitively,
for the first time, how easily
I could kill or be killed.

Murambi

Rwanda, 2008

There is no smell of death here. Even the lime
has faded from what it was meant to preserve.
Atop this hill, everything feels small and
possible. I convince myself school is out,
each classroom merely waiting. A holiday perhaps.
The grass, a twisted maze, yields sound
but no music. The battered doors, some still
stained a faint copper, were once tinged with
dark burgundy. When the breeze troubles
their rusty hinges, a pinched song overtakes
the concrete skeleton that remains, rises up
like a warning siren to anyone within earshot.
Midday rests an unrelenting blade against
our faces. A child on the abandoned soccer field
is full-out sprinting as though a stadium
full of souls is cheering him on.
Nothing here will ever again grow. His mother
is somewhere, getting water or gone. The guide,
who will not give me his name or ask for mine,
leads me to what every foreigner thinks
they came this far to see. They still use machetes
to cut the grass: *Among other things*, he reminds me,
it is a most useful instrument.

Abecedarian for the Pimp
I Almost Took a Bullet For

after Natalie Diaz

i.

All I knew at twenty-three was the two-sided coin:
bad & good, the world recast in a black & white
cinemascape. I wore a cheap knockoff from 1-2-5th—a
draped-loose bubble coat, my pockets choked with
everything I carried: condoms, brochures, business cards,
fragments of faded receipts (that would shower out with each
grab at my baggy jeans), my wallet & keys. At first, I
had two thoughts walking into the brothel: I need a new job &
I do not want to die. I still taste the punch of cheap incense, still
jump a little when I hear anything steel lock into place.
Kids would play on the mangled sidewalk out front,
leave their toys three stories beneath a chorus of rehearsed
moans scored to an escalating percussion of thumps.
Not once before had I seen a john in the lobby, until that day.
Out of nowhere, an argument swayed the bolted door open,
Papá turned to *Puto*, turned six-eight pimp with the
quickness, turning slurred words into a blur of bloodied
rings & bucked knuckles. *I'm nobody*, I told myself. *I'm a*
social worker, not some Good Samaritan & shit.
That is, until I caught a glimpse of the glinted metal
unveiled mid-spat from the john's backpack—overtaken by
visceral momentum, I tackled the skinny sap
with all of my weight, hoping my grip would hold.

ii.

X was a pimp once too. Murdered not too far from here.
You always laughed at the jokes on instinct, while the
zebra-printed miniskirt of a girl crouched low—out of sight.

Before the Last Shot

What was I doing at fifteen?
Facedown on the pavement,
nostrils tinged with bullet-smoke,
the brick-dust falling around
us like fresh snow (or white
chalk), his lanky silhouette stalking
the abandoned sidewalk.
It was summer, Brooklyn.
Nothing ever happens
until it happens. That's how my brother
and sister-in-law were describing
their tours in Iraq after our dinner
in Manhattan. We had decided to take
a shortcut through Sumner projects, then
heard the unmistakable sound that tore
through the story I was telling about
a lunchtime fight on the blacktop of
my high school, a sudden flash
of lightning. No one believed it
was happening. They forgot their army
training, rubber-necked towards
the source of the thunder. And then we
tumbled behind the parked cars.
Waited. For what, we were not sure.

Between cars, I could only make
out his narrow back and the dark
steel clutched in his small hands.
I needed to see his face, half
expecting to see myself: standing
on that corner aiming at
something that is never quite there.

There were Two Unanswered
Voice Mails from You

as a white sparrow, trapped inside the heated chamber
of Terminal 3 in O'Hare, zipped past ceiling vents no one
usually sees, while I furiously tried to rebook a flight to nowhere.
Months had slipped by since I last saw you, yet there you were:
wind-chapped grin rising from your favorite chartreuse turtleneck,
early-love smitten, seemingly mid-joke, staring down at
something just out of view. I needed to know what you saw.
Sometimes I convince myself I called you back, left
a long message that got cut off, that I stopped by your
door with artichoke hummus. When I first found out
you had AIDS, I prepared for what I would do
when you left. Then, you didn't. It seemed like a gag
we were all in on. An endless joke: death.
But survival is a chameleon—that softly
says *Carpe Noctem* while the knives are still coated
with fresh lime just a short reach from the old, beat-up tub.
I never understood just how carefully your shadow stalked you
each and every second you somehow found a way to live.

Race was not a factor,

they said. He said, *It*
looked like a demon. It
charged me like I was five, It
Hulk Hogan—

        two legacies
ghost-stenciled into concrete, one shadow
sifted into ash. He sleeps at night—*No*
regrets. His family as certain as the closed lid
of a coffin
they will be safe.

            It happened, he says. *It was*
unfortunate. It is
what It is.

      Which is the invisible
legacy—
        eighteen years of a boy's
stifled blush, choreography
of a scowl with index & middle
salute, sinew flung forward, barrel
chest soft as unmixed concrete, whisker-less
chin line. His crown was bursting
forth & bowed, inverted king
posing for a peon graced with steel, skull
twice knighted by fire. The final blade
of light cut endless through the high

frequency shrill that fluttered
from his mouth, dull thud from the brim
of a broached squeal. Because child. Because
scared. Because tired. The boy was done
with being shadow, dust film on boot
lip—wanted to be luminous. Sometimes a life
splinters to break. To scatter.
To be.

*

I see my nephew pressed to the edge
of boyhood, though he looks a man
in my imagination with his flinch
& blush muted, he is still
carved raw from the giggle that over-
takes his toddler body. Thomas
the Tank Engine is this moment's alibi
for letting go. As I watch him now
I see him still in that faded-cobalt,
whale-imprinted bib he kept soaked
through, but also, I see the son
I have now, knowing there is no plan.
    The nights   accrue
like gravestones in a tiny plot of land, like light-
less hallways that encircle the earth, an end-
less tether that yokes the crisp dusk from each
day as it is drained of light: what can never

be seen cast against what can never be
unseen. The promises made against
that other unspoken promise, grief,
made invisible beneath the shadow
of something too large to see—how all
our children share the same erased
name because of it. What leaves them
riddled with everything they cannot see:
piercing   &   rigid   &   always more
weight than anyone predicts. The child
still in the street. It is two minutes & a few
seconds past noon on Canfield Drive
in Ferguson, Missouri, & he is still
right there, in the middle
of the street. Not my nephew. Not my
son.

Father

i.

In the basement of the crack house   I used to visit
as an outreach worker   on 121st street in Harlem,
I was convinced   He   refused
to travel north of 96th.   I wrote a letter
to Joanna on her mission   in Taiwan, detailed
each irrefutable   piece of evidence   proving
we are all,   in fact,   alone.
Told her about   the nine-year-old orphan
forced   to sell   her body
for three years   before ending up   just off
Times Square,   discarded   in a dumpster.
I told her about   the eldest son
who answered   a burglar's call   and was shot,
paralyzed   from the waist down.   I asked her
about drought   and famine   and endless
civil wars—what lessons   does His book
refuse?

ii.

When her heart rate   dropped by half   in less
than a minute,   the population   of our cramped
hospital room   tripling   in a handful of seconds,
I grasped for   anything   that would keep me
upright.   At first,   the wall: cool and steady,
demanding my body   ascend beyond   what seemed
possible.   Then,   nothing,
no one.   I stood   in the waiting room
of the OR,   waiting   to be called in,
to find out if   my child   had survived.
I spent each second   trying to pull tiny shoe-coverings
over my too-large feet.   I confessed   every wrong
of my life   to an empty, over-lit room   of steel
and sterile instruments   that all   reflected back
distorted   versions of myself.   I fumbled
for any prayer   I could remember, hoping
that I had all along been   mistaken   about the hollow
blackness   of the infinite sky.   I never wanted
so badly   to have been wrong
about anything   in my life—

                         and then   a disembodied
     voice   called out,   seemingly only to me—
          a tiny growl   at first   that blossomed
          into a wail   dwarfing any thought   my mind
          could   possibly   hold,   any faith
          I'd ever been   so foolish   to claim.

Morning, Rikers Island

Physics and light
pierce the hollow stench
of the forgotten gymnasium
stripped naked of clocks.

All the adolescent boys
stop—offer their grief
to each other like water,
glancing out the only window
they all share. A single ray
unfolds its warmth
across the dusty belly
of the thudded parquet,
and here's the miracle:
the sun frees everyone
to sing.

Acknowledgments

Grateful acknowledgment is made to the editors of the following publications in which these poems, sometimes in earlier versions, first appeared:

Backbone Press	"Hijito"
BuzzFeed Reader	"What Happened"
Crab Creek Review	"Pronounced"
North American Review	"There were Two Unanswered Voice Mails from You"
Painted Bride Quarterly	"Black Hair" & "Morning, Rikers Island"
Paterson Literary Review	"The Afternoon You Moved Out"
Philadelphia Stories	"Murambi" & "*Race was not a factor*"
Smartish Pace	"Kigali Memorial" & "*Mein Kampf* has better reviews than *One Hundred Years of Solitude*"
Solstice Literary Magazine	"Before the Last Shot"
Southword Journal	"Abecedarian for the Pimp I Almost Took a Bullet For"
The Ocotillo Review	"Edge of the Dance Floor"

"Pronounced" also appears in the anthology *Ink Knows No Borders: Poems of the Immigrant and Refugee Experience* (Seven Stories Press, 2019).

None of these poems would have been possible without my mentors in the MFA Program for Writers at Warren Wilson College, in particular: C. Dale Young, Rodney Jones, Gabrielle Calvocoressi, Sandra Lim, Roger Reeves, Matthew Olzmann, Debra Allbery, and, of course, Ellen Bryant Voigt.

There are too many cherished loved ones who have held me up to thank personally here (that could be another book in itself), but a special shoutout to my dear Angel Nafis, for being my sister and support throughout grad school and beyond.

About the Author

Carlos Andrés Gómez is a Colombian American poet from New York City. He is the author of *Hijito* (Platypus Press, 2019), selected by Eduardo C. Corral as the winner of the 2018 Broken River Prize, and the memoir *Man Up: Reimagining Modern Manhood* (Penguin Random House, 2012). Winner of the *Atlanta Review* International Poetry Prize, Lucille Clifton Poetry Prize, and the Sandy Crimmins National Prize for Poetry, Gómez's writing has appeared, or is forthcoming, in the *New England Review*, *Beloit Poetry Journal*, *The Yale Review*, *BuzzFeed Reader*, *CHORUS: A Literary Mixtape* (Simon & Schuster, 2012), and elsewhere. Carlos is a graduate of the University of Pennsylvania and the MFA Program for Writers at Warren Wilson College.

*

For more, please visit: CarlosLive.com

Connect with Carlos on Twitter & Instagram: @CarlosAGLive

Find more poetry & prose
from Platypus Press at:

platypuspress.co.uk